A SHELL OF A LOT OF GRATITUDE

For the Times We Need to be Reminded

FRED WERTZ

Published by AuthorHouse 10/25/2012

ISBN: 978-1-4634-2380-3 (sc)

This book is printed on acid-free paper.

Because of the dynamic nature of the Internet, any web addresses or links contained in this book may have changed
since publication and may no longer be valid. The views expressed in this work are solely those of the author and do not
necessarily reflect the views of the publisher, and the publisher hereby disclaims any responsibility for them.

authorHOUSE®

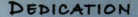

DEDICATION

    I dedicate this inspiration in hopes of enlightening those that love and tolerate me to have a Grateful day!

    I am most grateful for God's gift of my children: my beautiful and insightful daughter Kalindi, my strong and dedicated son Zack, their sister the creative and sensitive Govinda, their mother Kevala who brought them into this world , motivated and energetic Michelle and the newest...my amazing grandson Titus,

    Most recently my beautiful sweetheart Sunii who's smile and realness lighten up my life every day, her girls Alyssa and Savanna whom I am just beginning to know their strengths and beauties, of course my faithful buddy Smokey and all of our dogs Lucy, Mia and Oden.
All of which are proof that the Power of Attraction is working for and within me.

    Final thanks to Seashells.com for allowing me to use their beautiful images.

I am Grateful for Gratitude because...

GRATITUDE

Deepest love and appreciation from within for all that
is, all that has been and all that will be.
A feeling of thankfulness and appreciation.
An elusive feeling as we have so many things to
be grateful for and we do not realize it.

My favorite gratitude quote!

Introduction (How This Came To Be)

"Decide what you want"

"Believe you can have it"

"Believe you deserve it"

"Believe it is possible for you"

"And then close your eyes every day for several minutes

and visualize having what you already want and

feeling the feelings of already having it"

"Come out of that and focus for what you are grateful for already"

-Jack Canfield

I have lived most of my life as I am sure most of us have: stuck in the future and the past and have always had a difficult time being grateful in the moment.

One winter day I had an amazing moment of clarity as I was struggling to find my path. Intuitively, I have always known that spiritually and physically we are all one energy and that I could attract what I need and deserve into my life, but I just forget. I would go years between moments of clarity and now I realize that the element missing was "Gratitude". I desperately needed to remind myself of what I have to be grateful for on a daily if not momentary instance if I were going to live the life I was meant to live.

In my bored and lonely, yet brief time off, I started to take escapes to the Northern California sea shore. I had always gravitated towards the familiarity of the mountains, but in these times I had no time to travel that far so I figured I would learn to appreciate the sea as well. I started to find cool places to collect sea shells; I cherished my shells as treasures. I grew to also cherish these beautiful coves, rocks and sands as my new home and grounding place.

One day I had an inspired thought to write things that I am grateful for on each shell to remind me of all the great things in life that I have to be grateful for. I called these my "gratitude shells" and placed them in a very prominent place in my tiny home with my family pictures. Every time I pass this table I am reminded of all the great and glorious things I have to be grateful for in my everyday life.

In the next few weeks I had a confirming realization of how the power of attraction once again has worked in my life. It had been a grueling and lonely couple of months working exceptionally long days. I needed reviving so I escaped work early one sunny spring day. I ran home, grabbed my faithful and lonely dog Smokey and drove west in a daze for the drive to my sanity at the ocean's shore. As I drove in a state of exhaustion and confusion, I was thinking about my gratitude shells and thinking that I needed to find a new beach as the spots that I love, just do not seem to have many shells.

On this day, I took a wrong turn and I ended up in a hidden, quaint little town called Bolinas. It was so close yet so far away. I just kept driving on a dirt road that seemed to head no where. Miles from anywhere I chanced to spot a single trail weaving through the poison oak. I grabbed Smokey and headed down the path.

When I reached the bottom of the narrow and slippery path I was amazed to find a beach that stretched as far as I could see. It was walled on one side by the steep coastal cliffs carved for centuries by the tides and ferocious storms. The other edge of the shore was scattered with tide pools large and small. It was so beautiful! Smokey and I walked along the beach with the sun bathing our faces and just marveled in the secluded beauty for what seemed an eternity. When I came to my senses, I realized that there were more beautiful shells scattered amongst the seaweed and rocks than I had ever seen. In no time at all, Smokey and I had found dozens of shells and I just started writing my list of gratitudes on each shell right on the beach. This is when I realized that this quest to gather shells of gratitude was to be more than a basket full of shells with writing on them so I started to call them my "Shell of a lot of Gratitude". After all, I have a hell of a lot of gratitude, and I put it on shells!

After weeks of gathering shells and collecting my inspirations of gratitude, I started to take notes to explain why I am grateful for the inspirations on the shells and really started to feel that I had a gift to be shared.

Once confident enough, I shared my inspiration to make the "Shell of a lot of Gratitude" to my daughter Kalindi. She immediately expressed that these shells should be shared and given away in some manner. I was speechless as it has taken me decades to fully appreciate the premise of sharing in the power of attraction and she had it in an instant. I have learned in my readings that in order to attract positive outcomes, we must have positive thoughts and intentions and in order to attract, we must be willing to give. She nailed it with her simple statement; "in order for one to fully appreciate the gratitude and attract more into our lives we must be willing in turn to give our gratitude to another."

The closer you look, the more you will realize that everything in your life is a cause for gratitude.

In sharing my inspiration, I sincerely hope that you take what you want, interpret it to fit you and be enlightened by the rest!

I am Grateful for **Existence** because...

x

Existence

"To be or not to be- that is the question."
-William Shakespeare

"To be here now"
Your spirit, your soul and your earthly body.
This is the greatest of my gratitude.
The alternative is to not exist, to not be here.
Live your life to the fullest
grateful for every moment and be whatever you can be!

I am Grateful for **Breath of Life** because...

The Breath of Life

You are alive.

Alive to read this, alive to breathe, to think, to wonder, to hear, to see, to feel joy, to feel sorrow, to feel pain, to feel ecstasy, to touch, to smell, to love, to experience success, to experience failure, to laugh, to cry, to sweat, to shiver, to run, to crawl, to learn, to teach.

To be grateful for every thing whether it appears to be significant or not, just be grateful to have the opportunity to experience it.

I am Grateful for **Hope** because...

HOPE

There is hope for us all. It may seem fleeting and in despair,
but with faith there is hope. The more we can be grateful
for what we have in life, the more we can have hope.
If we have hope we can have dreams and this is our destiny!

I am Grateful for **Love** because...

Love

Be grateful for love like your life depends on it! It does. Every human being is capable of giving and receiving love no matter how alone and destitute you may feel. From the love for a person, creature, place, thing, activity or season. This realization of the beauty of this emotion will give you hope and purpose of life! Love is everything as so many popular songs will tell you. But really, love is what keeps us alive, love keeps us going, growing and glowing. Our deepest emotions of love are the most powerful vibrations for a world of harmony.

I am Grateful for **Peace** beca

Peace

Peace in the world, peace of mind, peace at one's existence.
With peace in our existence we are able to function and rest assured that
we are safe and secure and that innocent people are not being sacrificed.
Peace of mind allows us to focus on what is truly important
in our lives so that we can exist in a world of harmonic
balance between ourselves and our universe.

Be grateful for peace!

I am Grateful for **Family** because...

FAMILY

Many say that we do not pick our family, but I do not feel that to be true. As families we attract each other to one another far before our earthbound births. For some karmic reason we have been placed here to live and grow together. Regardless of whether you are getting along in the moment, your family is precious; you have far more in common than you may ever realize. You have the same roots, the same memories, both good and bad and you are meant to work it out together. Do not wait until it is too late to appreciate and be grateful for your family!!

I am Grateful for **Daughters** because...

Daughters

"You are so beautiful to me,

Can't you see,

You're everything I hoped for,

You're everything I dreamed,

You are so beautiful to me"

-Joe Cocker

What else can I say?

If you have daughters, you know what I mean!

13

I am Grateful for **Sons** because...

14

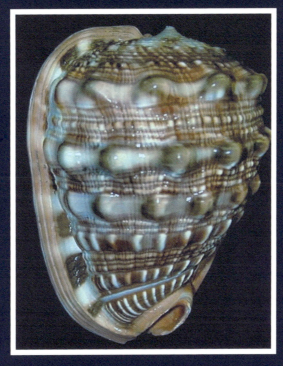

Sons

Spiders and snakes, rocks and mud, legos and kinex, cars and trucks, skateboards and snowboards, footballs, soccer balls and wrestling shoes, books and video games, boy to man, buddy and friend, athlete, scholar or chef. Just as daughters are so beautiful so are sons in a different way. They just may not want to be labeled as such.

I am Grateful for **Mothers** because...

MOTHERS

Mothers are one of our most precious things to be grateful for. Your mother gave you her womb, her blood, her spirit and soul to protect and nourish you until God was ready for you to emerge into the world. Then she endured the most intense pain and pressure to push you out. Believe it or not she has continued and will continue with this dedication and love until the passing of time.

I am Grateful for **Fathers** because...

18

FATHERS

I did not know mine... wish I did, but always tried to be a good one.

To me, a father is someone that you can count on, the foundation,

the cornerstone and the trusted one that is always there.

Some loud, some quiet, some involved, some not so much. All very much

a part of our lives at least spiritually if not emotionally and physically.

I am Grateful for **Brothers** because...

20

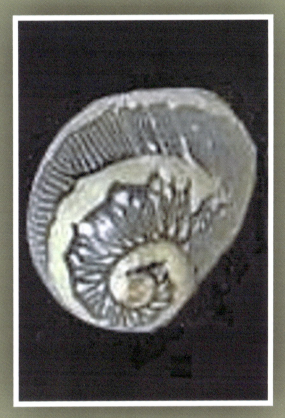

BROTHERS

Big brothers or little brothers all turn out to be amiable, protectors, pain in the asses, quiet, loud, big and little, lights in your life. They teach you, they guide you, they enable you to teach and guide and they have more in common with you than almost anybody else. Love them, cherish them and share your strengths, hopes, dreams and disappointments together. Brothers stick with you.

I am Grateful for **Sisters** because...

Sisters

Big sisters, little sisters, twin sisters, step sisters. Friend, foe, rival, partner, sisters are always there for you, always aware of you. They know everything and appear to know nothing. They start out like a mother one day and then throw rocks at you the next. Such is a sister.

I am Grateful for **Pets** because...

Pets

Dogs, cats, birds, hamsters, rats.
Pets are such great friends. They are always happy to see you and
will never tell your secrets. So reliant and yet so independent.
We think that we choose our pets and this is just not true. We
have a karmic relationship or bond with our pets. We are together;
we are here for one another as we need them just as much as they
need us. Love them, care for them and be grateful for them.

I am Grateful for **Friends** because...

26

FRIENDS

BFF, homie. Buddy, pal, comrade, partner, friend forever. We get to choose our friends on a karmic and physical level. Friends are companions that share our interests, likes, dislikes, hopes, dreams and aspirations. Friends are there through thick and thin to support, embrace or just hang. "Making Friends for all the world to see"

-Elton John

I am Grateful for **Mentors** because...

Mentors

Whether they know it or not, mentors are the ones that guide us by example. Look around you and see the ones that have lead you and especially see the ones that you lead. We are all mentors to someone. Be careful and appreciate everything you do as you are mentoring someone.

I am Grateful for **Acknowledgement** because...

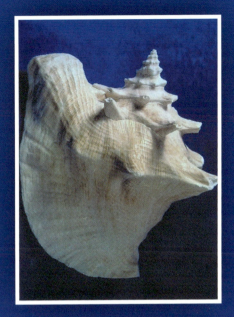

ACKNOWLEDGEMENT

To be acknowledged means to exist. If you are acknowledged for any little thing it gives you reason to feel significance in this universe. It means that on the pure energy level that you are connected and therefore can practice the power of attraction. A smile, a nod, a wink, a handshake, a glance. I am grateful for my existence and to be recognized and acknowledged.

"...that the tiniest gesture -- a smile, a gentle look, a simple pat on the arm, a soft word -- can change a person's life."

-Neale Donald Walsch

31

I am Grateful for **Vivid Clarity** because...

Vivid Clarity

What the hell is that?

We think it will never happen but

at some point in life we all wake up at least once with a

vivid clarity of who we are and why we are here.

Please do not wait for your death bed- be here now and be grateful

for every ever-so-slight glimpses of clarity in your life.

I am Grateful for **Harmony** because...

HARMONY

To be **in** harmony with the universe is to be **one** with the universe.
All of the beauty and turmoil, the astonishment and the
mundane. To be in harmony is to be in tune with one's connection,
purpose, destiny and dreams as they relate to all others.

I am Grateful for **Integrity** because...

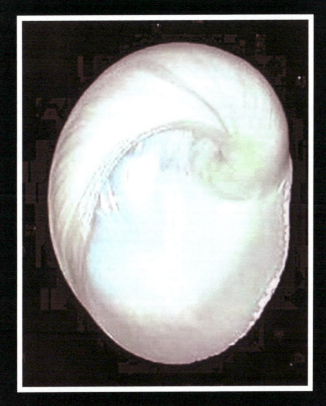

Integrity

What do we have in this lifetime but to be true to one's
self, one's beliefs, to another living soul...?
To be trusted to do the "right thing". To keep one's word,
to be counted on to be there when needed.
I am grateful for other's integrity as well as my own.

I am Grateful for **a Smile** because...

40

A SMILE

A beautiful and personal gesture to give and to receive.
The physical expression of pleasure, joy and acceptance.
A quick glimpse, a cordial greeting, brief acknowledgment
and acceptance, ending in a relaxed and meaningful
smile is such a simple, yet meaningful encounter.

I am Grateful for **Laughter** because...

LAUGHTER

The outward and verbal expression of joy and humor as the side bursts out is the sound and expression of laughter. To many the sound of laughter is but a dream, a faint memory of a time that has passed. It is essential to celebrate the humor that life has to offer no matter how minute or ironic.

I am Grateful for **Music** because...

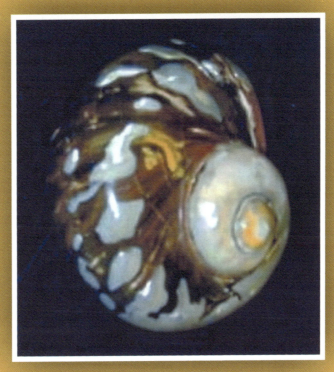

Music

Soothing, relaxing, exhilarating.

Such sweet music to my ears

Music can tame wild beasts, put babies to sleep, lead great marches
and influence a generation. Music can make your mood. If in a mood,
merely change the music to change that mood. Music can uplift spirits,
bring back memories and if nothing else, pick up the tempo of the day.

"Don't let it bring you down"

-The Beatles

I am Grateful for **Wishes** because...

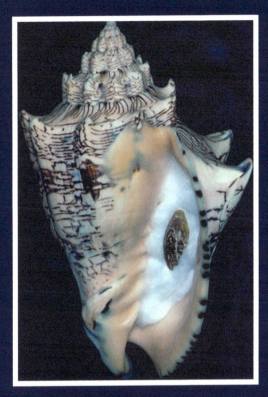

WISHES

Children wish upon a star, upon a dandelion, upon the tooth fairy. As we grow older and wiser we lose our childish nature and forget to wish. James Ray claimed that Aladdin did not have 3 wishes, but that he had uncountable wishes and in our universe we too have uncountable wishes through the power of attraction. So I say be grateful for life and start wishing for a brighter future for us all.

I am Grateful for **Faith** because...

48

FAITH

Faith in God, faith in another, faith that the sun will rise, faith
that we will grow old. Faith gives us hope and appreciation that
we shall continue to live, to breathe and to fulfill our destiny.

I am Grateful for **The Gift** because...

The Gift

God gave us all a great gift in our existence and a purpose. I am grateful that God gave me the gift to share strength, insight and hope to the world with gratitude through our power of attraction.

I am Grateful for **Sensory Memory** because...

SENSORY MEMORY

I am very grateful for my sensory memory. The senses are a wondrous thing. Ever smell mothballs and remember Grandmas house and her love and care? How about the smell of incense and your favorite poster shop as a teenager, or the taste of some exotic cuisine that you tasted with a long lost love? My favorite is music, oh wow, how I go back in time when I hear songs that bring back the first dance, the first kiss, the first record or concert, the first drive. When life gets heavy and I can't find much to be grateful for, I pull the Sensory Memory Shell and of course the MP3 and before long I am back on track, confident and feeling warm inside!!!

I am Grateful for **Ambition** because...

AMBITION

To grow, to excel, to prosper, to be one with the universe.
Ambition of spirit, of purpose and of self.
To be ambitious is to be willing to work and strive
to fulfill and follow your dreams.
Ambition is what carries the momentum for growth.

I am Grateful for **Youth** because...

Youth

Don't for a minute change where you're at in life. Most of us spend our youth trying to be grown up and not fully appreciating how great youth is and how wonderful all of the firsts of life are. It is our greatest gift to be able to transform ourselves to be young at heart by having gratitude for what we have and how we have helped others.

I am Grateful for **Curiosity** because...

CURIOSITY

The inspiration of creativity and invention!

We think: "what if"

When pondering how something works or how something will look

"if" you change it. Children are the masters of innocent curiosity

as they scurry around the day asking what, why, where and how.

I am so grateful for God's gift of curiosity in mankind.

So... "WHAT IF"?

I am Grateful for **Flirtation** because...

FLIRTATION

Who doesn't love and appreciate a little flirtation?
Subtle, sensual, lingering, exciting, and erotic. As it fills the senses,
they tingle, the mind wonders and the spirit attracts. Flirtation gives
one an appreciation and gratitude to be noticed and attractive to another.

I am Grateful for **Intelligence** because...

INTELLIGENCE

As human beings we are gifted with intelligence. We have been given the capacity to communicate, to make decisions, to solve puzzles, to figure things out, to plan, to design and to use tools. How could you not be grateful for your intelligence and the intelligence of others?

I am Grateful for **Creativity** because...

CREATIVITY

To outwardly express ones designs, talents, ideas, plans
and layouts in an attractive and original manner.
If it were not for the creativity of God and man, we would
live in a flat, black and white universe. I am grateful
for every creative idea that I have ever had.

I am Grateful for **Blankets** because...

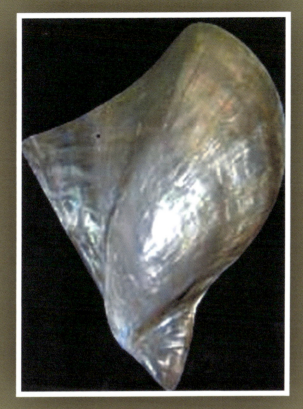

BLANKETS

Taken so much for granted by many. A blanket is probably
the world's most reliable source of warmth and protection.
From the moment we leave the womb until the moment we leave this
earthly body, we will always find comfort in a warm blanket.

I am Grateful for **Sex** because...

Sex

I will be careful on this one just in case my adult
offspring actually read this far.
Be grateful for the ability and any opportunity you have to
have sex...this beautiful bond should not be taken for granted...
just look at the really young adults and really old ones too,
they are grateful for any chance and the ability to get any.
Strange coincidence or not, we must not forget this!

I am Grateful for **Intimacy** because...

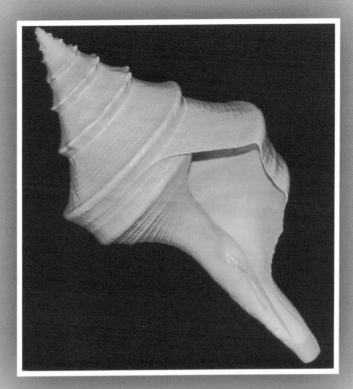

INTIMACY

Not necessarily to be confused with sex.
As human beings we are capable and blessed with the ability to be close,
to touch, to feel, to talk to express deep emotional and physical love in
intimacy. The feeling and bond shared by two is taken for granted
by many until it is gone. We all need intimacy in our lives even if we
deny it. Please appreciate even the fleeting moments of intimacy.

I am Grateful for **Serenity** because...

SERENITY

God grant me the serenity to
Accept the things I cannot change;
courage to change the things I can;
and wisdom to know the difference.
Living one day at a time;
Enjoying one moment at a time;
Accepting hardships as the pathway to peace;
Taking, as He did, this sinful world
as it is, not as I would have it;
Trusting that He will make all things right
if I surrender to His Will;
That I may be reasonably happy in this life
and supremely happy with Him
Forever in the next.

-Reinhold Niebuhr

I am Grateful for **The Power of Attraction** because...

POWER OF ATTRACTION

The energy and source of our needs, desires, hopes and dreams. It is the link in the universe and the realization that we are all comprised of the same energy and source with all of creation. By resonating this energy in positive harmony with the universe we can attract what we need and strive for in life. If we live in a place of negative energy we will attract negative outcomes. If we live in a place of positive energy, we will attract positive things into our lives. Everything we could ever need or want is already in existence in the universe, we just need to attract it into our current existence by "being here now."

I am so grateful that I consciously discovered the power of attraction. I have always had a very powerful attractive talent and did not know it. I have attracted great things into my life as obviously I attracted my beautiful family and pets into my life. I have also attracted some negative energy of being helpless and a victim but no more as is our family tradition. Once I subconsciously made the decision to do something about it I attracted people into my life that could teach me.

The greatest lesson that I can give is that in order to attract greater things into our lives we must be grateful for what we have. If we dwell in a place of dissatisfaction with our lives, our homes, our jobs, our cars… I think you see where I am going, we will attract the same. As they say "the definition of insanity is continuing the same insane actions and expecting a different outcome. So let's get into a positive place of gratitude, realize that you have already attracted miracles and share this new power and insight with everybody that you come across!!!!

I would like to close with a quote by one of the most influential individuals in human history:

"As we express our gratitude, we must never forget that the highest appreciation is not to utter words, but to live by them."

-John F. Kennedy

"Have a Grateful Day"

Fred

CPSIA information can be obtained
at www.ICGtesting.com
Printed in the USA
LVIW011012161112

307404LV00001BA